FLORATORIUM

By Joanne Oppenheim • Illustrated by S. D. Schindler

With an introduction by Catherine Eberbach, Science Consultant

A Byron Preiss Book

BANTAM BOOKS

NEW YORK • TORONTO • LONDON • SYDNEY • AUCKLAND

To Sarah, who helped smooth a path through the forest
—J.O.

FLORATORIUM

A Bantam Book/April 1994

Series graphic design by Alex Jay/Studio J
Senior Editor: Sarah Feldman
Assistant Editor: Kathy Huck
Special thanks to Betsy Gould, William H. Hooks, Hope Innelli,
James A. Levine, Ellen Schecter, and Howard Zimmerman.

Library of Congress Cataloging-in-Publication Data

Oppenheim, Joanne.
Floratorium/Joanne Oppenheim;
illustrated by S.D. Schindler;
with an introduction by Catherine Eberbach.
p.   cm. – (A Bank street museum book)
"A Byron Preiss book."
Includes index.
Summary: Uses a tour through
a botanical museum to introduce
many different kinds of plants
and the ways in which they
grow all over the world.
ISBN 0-553-09365-7.   –   ISBN 0-553-37145-2
1. Botanical museums—Juvenile literature.   [1. Plants.
2. Botany.   3. Botanical museums.]   I. Schindler, S.D., ill.
II. Title.   III. Series.
QK79.066 1994
581 – dc20
92-17886
CIP
AC

Published simultaneously in the United States and Canada

PRINTED IN THE UNITED STATES OF AMERICA

0 9 8 7 6 5 4 3 2 1

Introduction

As a young child I followed my father and grandfather on Sunday inspections of the garden. Smelling sweet williams, finding the pale yellow of a Peace rose, hearing the first bees of spring, and climbing our big oak tree are memories I still cherish. When I moved away from home, I missed my father's garden, and in no time my apartment became a virtual greenhouse, with plants spilling from windowsills and bookshelves; I've gardened ever since.

Understanding plants and the ecosystems in which they live is basic to understanding life on earth. An ecosystem is essentially made up of living and nonliving parts that interact with each other. The Sonoran desert is one kind of ecosystem and the Arctic tundra is another. But cities and towns are also ecosystems; an ecosystem is not just *out there*—it's right where you live.

Plants have an important role to play in the well-being of people, and people influence the balance of ecosystems. Plants provide oxygen to all living things and are sources of food, shelter, and clothing. People influence the development and survival of ecosystems because they are a part of ecosystems themselves; destabilizing an ecosystem threatens the survival of a diversity of plant and animal species. The more experience with and knowledge about plants and ecosystems you have, the more you will discover how important they are to your daily and future life.

Today, many young people are concerned about the environment; they worry about the destruction of tropical rain forests, the pollution of waterways, and holes in the ozone. Only when people see themselves as part of an ecosystem can they speak about living responsibly on this planet. Seeing *yourself* as part of the environment is the first step. So take a journey through the Floratorium and be part of the plant world. Afterward, go outside and smell the roses!

Catherine Eberbach
Children's and Family Programs
The New York Botanical Garden

HALL OF MAPS

Welcome to the Floratorium. Here in the museum you will see how plants grow in almost every part of the world—from the frozen arctic tundra to the steaming tropics, from the floor of the ocean to the roof of the forests, and across dry deserts and rolling prairies.

Take a moment to look at this model. It will give you a bird's-eye view of the museum.

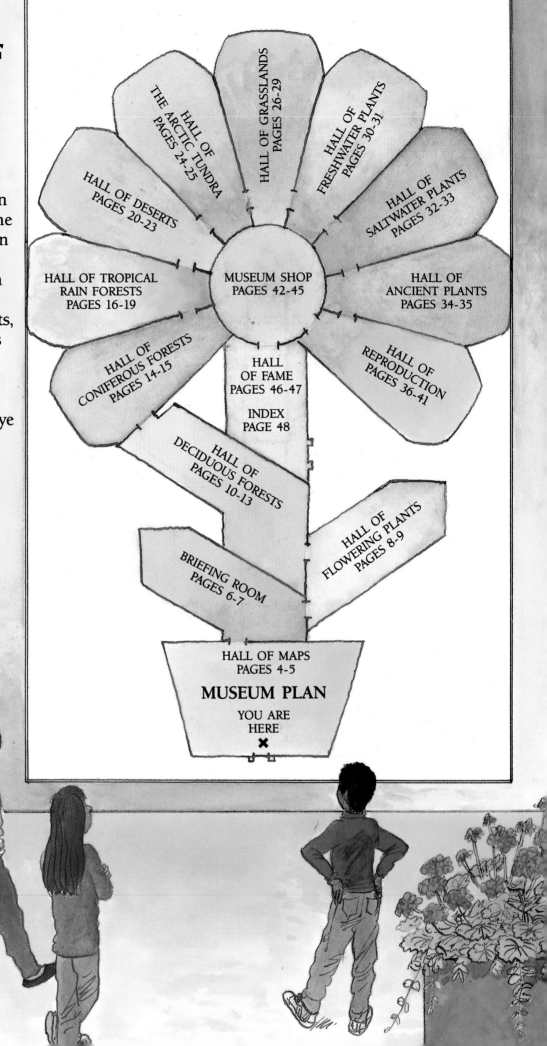

HALL OF THE ARCTIC TUNDRA
PAGES 24-25

HALL OF GRASSLANDS
PAGES 26-29

HALL OF FRESHWATER PLANTS
PAGES 30-31

HALL OF DESERTS
PAGES 20-23

HALL OF SALTWATER PLANTS
PAGES 32-33

HALL OF TROPICAL RAIN FORESTS
PAGES 16-19

MUSEUM SHOP
PAGES 42-45

HALL OF ANCIENT PLANTS
PAGES 34-35

HALL OF CONIFEROUS FORESTS
PAGES 14-15

HALL OF FAME
PAGES 46-47

INDEX
PAGE 48

HALL OF REPRODUCTION
PAGES 36-41

HALL OF DECIDUOUS FORESTS
PAGES 10-13

HALL OF FLOWERING PLANTS
PAGES 8-9

BRIEFING ROOM
PAGES 6-7

HALL OF MAPS
PAGES 4-5

MUSEUM PLAN

YOU ARE HERE
✗

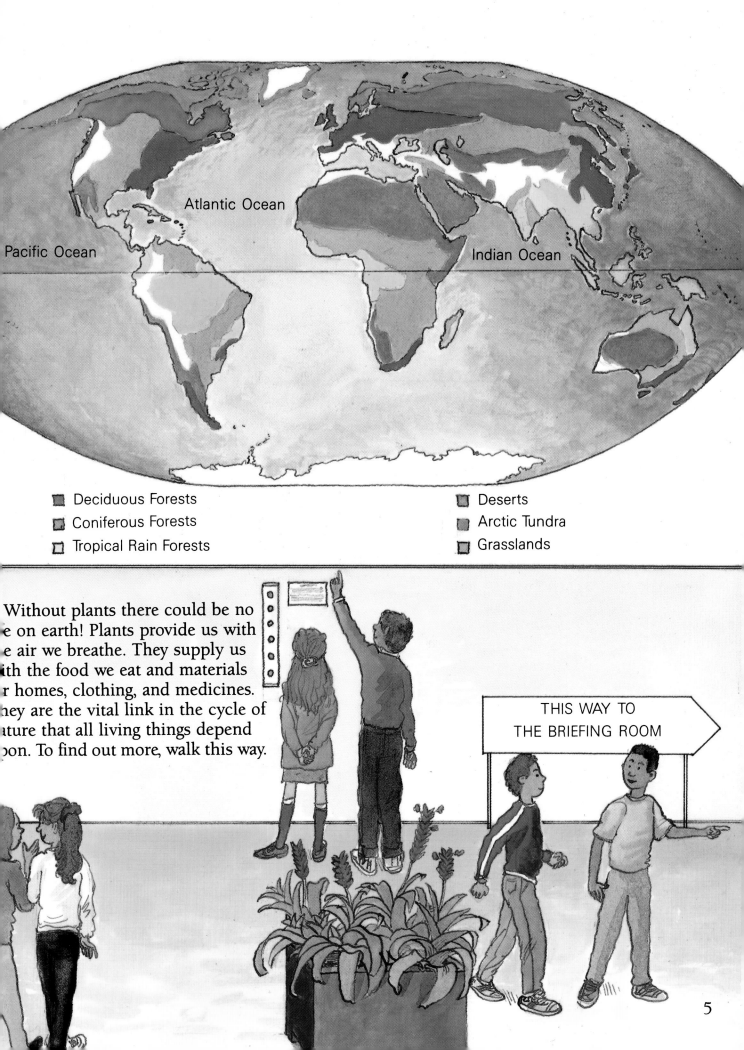

Pacific Ocean

Atlantic Ocean

Indian Ocean

- Deciduous Forests
- Coniferous Forests
- Tropical Rain Forests

- Deserts
- Arctic Tundra
- Grasslands

Without plants there could be no life on earth! Plants provide us with the air we breathe. They supply us with the food we eat and materials for homes, clothing, and medicines. They are the vital link in the cycle of nature that all living things depend upon. To find out more, walk this way.

THIS WAY TO
THE BRIEFING ROOM

BRIEFING ROOM

What Makes a Plant a Plant?

When you think of a plant, what do you picture? A green leafy stem with roots at the bottom and flowers on top? Although some plants do look like that, many do not.

In fact, some plants are neither green nor leafy. Simple plants such as algae and fungi have no true stems, roots, or leaves. Some plants are so small they can only be seen under a microscope. Others, such as the giant redwoods, are as big as a tall building.

Fungi are one of a group of plants including mushrooms and toadstools. They cannot make their own food because they do not contain chlorophyll, the substance that makes plants green. They get their food by living on other plants.

Algae are simple plants that live chiefly in water but also on rocks and on the bark of trees.

Lichens are a combination of an alga and a fungus. The alga supplies food for the fungus.

Lichens

Algae

HALL OF FLOWERING PLANTS

Flowering plants can be classified by the length of time they live. Many of the brightest summer flowers, such as petunias, are annuals. Others, such as hollyhocks, are biennials and bloom just once, in their second year. The longest-lasting plants are perennials, such as black-eyed Susans, which bloom year after year.

Annuals live until they produce seeds and die. New seeds must be planted each year.

Biennials live two years. In year 1, they grow leaves; in year 2, they flower and seed and then die.

Perennials continue to grow year after year. They make seeds annually and store food in their root system. The part above ground dies, but the roots continue to live.

YEAR 1

YEAR 1

YEAR 2

YEAR 1

YEAR 2

YEAR 3

Green leaves are often called the food factory. This is where most of the plant's food is made through the process of photosynthesis.

Flowers contain the reproductive parts of the plant.

Fruit develops from the flower and has seeds inside.

Tomato

Stem

water vapor out

carbon dioxide in

oxygen out

water

carbon dioxide

food stored

food stored

water

Process of Photosynthesis

Photosynthesis is the way green plants use sunlight, carbon dioxide, and water to make their own food. During the process, the plant releases oxygen and water vapor into the air.

Photosynthesis is the vital link in cleaning and recycling the air we breathe.

Stems support the leaves and carry water and minerals back and forth from roots to leaves. Photosynthesis also happens here.

THIS WAY TO DECIDUOUS FORESTS

Roots absorb water and minerals. They also hold the plant in the soil like an anchor.

HALL OF DECIDUOUS FORESTS

There are three main kinds of forests in the world – deciduous, coniferous, and tropical. Before we enter each of them, take a moment to look at how a forest changes over a long period of time.

Here in the deciduous forest the trees go from bare to leafy with the changing seasons.

In autumn, the trees shed their leaves and then rest all winter. In spring, their buds open and new leaves and flowers burst forth. Trees such as the oak, maple, beech, chestnut, hickory, and European mountain ash are just a few of the many kinds of trees that grow in deciduous forests.

The Birth of a Deciduous Forest

Step 1: Weeds and shrubs cover the wild meadow. Insects, mice, snakes, and birds live in the tall weeds. Pine seedlings are poking up here and there among the weeds.

Step 2: Pine seedlings grow into a young forest as they reach for the sun. Meanwhile, beneath the pines, young oak seedlings are taking root. The young pine seedlings need more light than they are getting.

10

Step 3: Now the oaks have grown taller than the old pines, which are dying. Young oaks are also growing but not the pine seedlings. They cannot live without light.

Step 4: This is now a mature forest, with no more pines, only leafy trees such as the oak. The forest will continue to change over time.

The canopy of the deciduous forest is generally about 100 feet tall. The trees of the canopy get full sunlight. Beneath the treetops, the forest is often dense with shrubs and other plants. Here the plants have two different growing seasons. Some flowering plants blossom in spring before the leaves of the tall trees blot out the sunlight. Others, such as shade plants, grow only in the cool darkness of the leafy summer forest.

Most deciduous forests grow in temperate areas, where the climate is mild. Winters are cold but summers are warm.

12

Beech

Ginkgo

Oak

Horse Chestnut

Maple

Hickory

European Mountain Ash

Leaves have many shapes, which help to identify the plant from which they come. In fall, the sap of the trees stops flowing and the chlorophyll, which makes the leaves green, dries. That's when the leaves turn colors and fall.

The underside of a leaf has tiny openings, or pores, called stomata. It's through these pores that gas enters the leaf, and gas and water leave the tree.

How many creatures can you find?

How many plants do you see?

THIS WAY TO CONIFEROUS FORESTS

Can you find a leaf that is shaped like a hand? Can you find a fan-shaped one?

HALL OF CONIFEROUS FORESTS

In the north, below the Arctic tundra, a vast forest of conifers encircles the world. It stretches across the northern parts of Eurasia and North America. Here the winters are extremely cold and the growing season is short.

Conifers—trees that bear cones—are especially well adapted to life in the cold north. Their needles are always ready to soak up the sun to make food. These needle-like leaves have fewer pores, or stomata, so they lose less water. Most conifers have sloping branches, so snow slides off. This protects trees from breaking under the weight of heavy snow.

Conifers also grow throughout the world in forests where there are deciduous trees.

Here's a thick layer of lichen growing on the tree trunks!

The oldest living plant on earth is a bristlecone pine. It is 4,600 years old and grows in California.

Experiment
Look for cones in the park or woods. Break them open—hold them upside down and tap. Do you find any seeds?

Coniferous forests grow in an uneven layer of trees that stand about 75 feet high. Only shade plants, such as ferns, mosses, and mushrooms, can grow on the dry sunless floor of the forest.

Pine

Fir

Yew

Cedar

Sequoia

Spruce

Conifers have various leaf shapes. Many, such as the pine, have long fine needles. The spruce has spiky needles. Others, such as the fir and yew, have flat needles. Still others, such as the cedar or giant sequoia, have tiny, scalelike needles.

Look at the cone I found.

Look at this huge moss growing on the floor of the forest!

THIS WAY TO TROPICAL RAIN FORESTS

HALL OF TROPICAL RAIN FORESTS

Nowhere on earth can you find as many kinds of plants as in a tropical rain forest. In the Amazon, there may be as many as 3,000 plant species in one square mile. Among the many rain forest trees are the bright-flowering cassias, cashews, mahoganies, rosewoods, balsas, and palms. Here trees can grow 15 feet in a year. Sixty to 100 inches of rain may fall annually, and there may be thunderstorms more than 200 days a year. Tropical rain forests release much of the oxygen we need to breathe. Unfortunately, people are destroying the rain forests at the rate of 88 acres a minute, and most of these forests will never grow again.

Toucan

Moth

Iguana

I thought it would be like a jungle with vines all over the ground.

No, the floor of the rain forest is almost free of green plants. Only a little sunlight can get through the thick trees.

Almost all tropical rain forests are near the equator. The three largest ones are in South America, Asia, and Africa.

Temperature: Averages 80° Fahrenheit with little change seasonally.

Emergent Trees

Marmoset

Hummingbird

Spider Monkey

Jaguar

Tapir

Tarantula

Upper Canopy

The rain forest grows in three main layers. The upper canopy grows about 150 feet tall. A few giants, called emergent trees, soar as high as 200 feet. This dense canopy forms the leafy umbrella of the forest. Here you will find the greatest number of plants and creatures.

Understory

The understory includes trees about 100 feet tall. They may grow into the upper canopy.

Lower Canopy

The trees of the lower canopy grow 50 to 60 feet tall and can survive in shade. Here palm trees and ferns spread their broad leaves, and tropical violets may grow as tall as an apple tree!

Trees must compete for sunlight and grow rapidly upward but have shallow roots. Some have developed buttressed roots to keep them from falling.

The forest floor is alive with fungi, tree seedlings, and insects. Leaves and dead animals decompose and enrich the soil.

Below ground, tarantulas burrow and leaf-cutting ants make gardens of fungi.

Most of the trees in the tropical rain forest are broad-leafed evergreens. Their branches are never bare. Leaves may live 13 to 14 months. When one leaf falls, another leaf replaces it at once.

Many of the other plants of the rain forest are "hitchhikers" that live on the tall trunks and leafy branches of the canopy, where there is the most light. Epiphytes (or air plants), such as orchids and bromeliads, never touch the ground. They live in treetops and absorb moisture from the air.

Some plants, such as lianas, start on the ground. These thick and twisting vines may be as thick as a person's waist. They climb rapidly toward the sun and weave their way through the treetops like a net.

Which one of these high climbers is a parasite that destroys the tree it climbs?

Orchid

Cacao

Bromeliads

Bromeliads are air plants. They can collect as much as 4½ quarts of water in their vaselike leaves, where tree frogs and beetles live.

Ceiba trees bear fruit pods with fluffy fibers that are used to stuff life jackets and cushions.

Orchids are the largest family of flowering plants. There are 25,000 known species of orchids and new ones are still being discovered.

Pitcher Plants attract insects with their scent and trap them inside their pitcher-shaped leaf. These carnivorous plants have special glands to digest their catch.

18

Strangler Fig

Pitcher Plant

Ceiba

Do you believe there are plants that trap insects?

Sure! They are called carnivorous plants.

Cacao grows to 40 feet in the wild. Cultivated plants grow to 25 feet. The fruit has a melon-shaped pod 12 inches long with seeds the size of lima beans. The seeds are used for chocolate, cocoa, and medicine.

Rafflesia is the largest flower in the world. Its flower may be 3 feet wide. The main part of the plant lives underground. Flies that pollinate it are attracted to its putrid odor, which smells like rotten meat.

Strangler Figs sprout up in the treetops and put out two kinds of roots. One root anchors to the tree, while the other creeps down to the soil. Eventually the fig takes over and the host tree rots!

Record Breaker: The wettest rain forest of the world is in Cherrapunji, India. It gets more than 400 inches of rain a year!

THIS WAY TO DESERTS

Rafflesia

HALL OF DESERTS

In the desert, plants must survive for long stretches of time with little or no water. Rain may not fall here for ten months or more. Plants of the desert do not grow close together because they must compete for water.

Basically, scientists divide desert plants into two main groups—those that resist the dry hot climate, and those that escape it.

Drought Escapers

Many of the most beautiful flowering desert plants lie dormant as seeds in the soil until the rain comes. Then, almost overnight, they carpet the desert with showy, scented flowers that soon produce new seeds. In 6 to 8 weeks the cycle is over and new seeds are scattered. They remain dormant until the next rain.

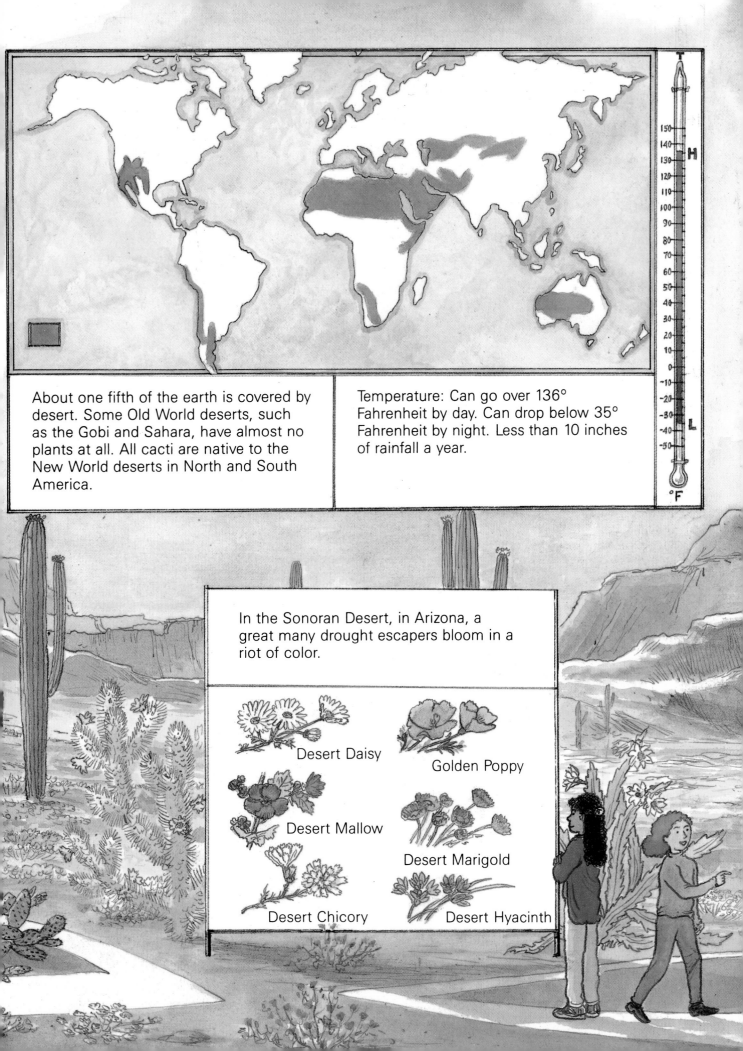

About one fifth of the earth is covered by desert. Some Old World deserts, such as the Gobi and Sahara, have almost no plants at all. All cacti are native to the New World deserts in North and South America.

Temperature: Can go over 136° Fahrenheit by day. Can drop below 35° Fahrenheit by night. Less than 10 inches of rainfall a year.

150
140
130
120
110
100
90
80
70
60
50
40
30
20
10
0
-10
-20
-30
-40
-50
°F

H

L

In the Sonoran Desert, in Arizona, a great many drought escapers bloom in a riot of color.

Desert Daisy

Golden Poppy

Desert Mallow

Desert Marigold

Desert Chicory

Desert Hyacinth

Drought Resisters

These plants have a variety of ways to survive. Cacti and other succulents can store water for long periods of time in their swollen stems and deep roots. Many desert plants also have thorns that protect them from animals and provide shade.

Many plants have shallow but wide-spreading roots. They can quickly catch and absorb a great amount of rain when it falls. Others, such as the night-blooming cereus, have a bulbous root shaped like a potato that stores water and food. Still others, such as the mesquite, have taproots that go as deep as 40 feet to search for a water supply.

Saguaro

Century Plant

Prickly Pear

Saguaro — the biggest cactus — grows only in the Sonoran Desert, and in parts of Mexico, Arizona, and California. It takes 50 years to flower, 75 years before branches appear, and can live 200 years growing more than 45 feet tall.

Barrel Cactus has curved spines that Native Americans used for fish-hooks. Its juicy pulp has saved thirsty travelers. It can also be used as a compass as it generally leans south.

Mesquite Trees have tiny leaves and may drop them in a drought. They store water in their stems. Young trees grow deep roots before the stem appears.

Joshua Trees live only at elevations above 2,500 feet, where summer is hot and winter is cold.

Century Plants are succulents that store water in their leaves. They reach a full height of 20 to 30 feet. People used to think they bloomed just once in 100 years, but that's not true. Some bloom annually.

Creosote Bushes grow 2 to 5 feet high and provide shade, food, and shelter for desert animals, and keep soil from eroding.

Prickly Pears grow along the ground in dry, rocky areas. They bear a pear-shaped, tasty fruit.

Jumping Chollas don't really jump, but stems fall off easily onto people and animals.

THIS WAY TO
THE ARCTIC TUNDRA

HALL OF THE ARCTIC TUNDRA

Here in the polar north is the cold, treeless desert called the Arctic tundra. The sunless days of winter last from September to May. When summer comes, the sun never sets and the tundra comes alive with plants and creatures.

Less than 10 inches of rain or snow fall each year. Most of the year the tundra is frozen solid. In spring a shallow layer of the surface (from 1 to 5 feet deep) begins to thaw. Then the hillsides and meadows burst into bloom. Plants of the tundra have wide but shallow roots and grow close to the ground, which protects them from the wind. Underground lies the permafrost, the solidly frozen ice that never melts.

Why aren't there any trees here?

Because of the permafrost, trees can't grow the deep roots they need to stand against the wind.

Crowberry

More than 100 kinds of flowering plants grow during the two short months of summer. Can you find the yellow arctic poppy? Purple monkshead? Blue lupine? Pink Lapland rosebay?

Arctic Cotton Grass

The Arctic tundra circles the north of America, Europe, and Asia. It lies between the frozen ice packs of the polar north and the tree line of the coniferous forests.

Temperature: In the summer, 31° to 54° Fahrenheit. In the winter, below 0° Fahrenheit.

Crowberry is one of many heath plants, including bearberry and cranberry. It has small tough leaves and grows in thick mats that collect the sun's rays. Air near these plants may be 20° Fahrenheit warmer than air above it.

Sphagnum Moss grows where it is too wet for lichens in wet, damp hollows. It is a soft plant that can be used as a diaper for babies.

Arctic Cotton Grass grows in the wetland of vast meadows. The tops of this short grass have distinctive white puffs.

Caribou Lichen is the most dominant plant of the Arctic. This brown and white plant has no leaves, roots, stem, or flowers and is the main food of the caribou. It grows slowly. One the size of your hand may be over 100 years old!

Cloudberry bears pale orange berries that look like rasberries but are not too tasty. This plant grows on edges of wetlands.

Caribou Lichen

Cloudberry

THIS WAY TO
THE GRASSLANDS

Sphagnum Moss

25

HALL OF GRASSLANDS
PRAIRIES OF NORTH AMERICA

When the covered wagons headed west in the 1800s, the prairie grasslands stretched from the Appalachians to the Rocky Mountains. These vast and nearly treeless fields looked like a "sea of grass" to the settlers. In the east, the moist prairie grass was tall and thick. Going westward toward the desert, the grass was shorter and grew in clumps.

Over the years, the wild and natural grasslands have been turned into farms and ranches. Here cereal grains and grasses such as wheat, oats, corn, and barley are grown to feed people and livestock.

There are grasslands on every continent except Antarctica!

Yes, but they all have different names: the pampa, steppe, savanna, and prairie.

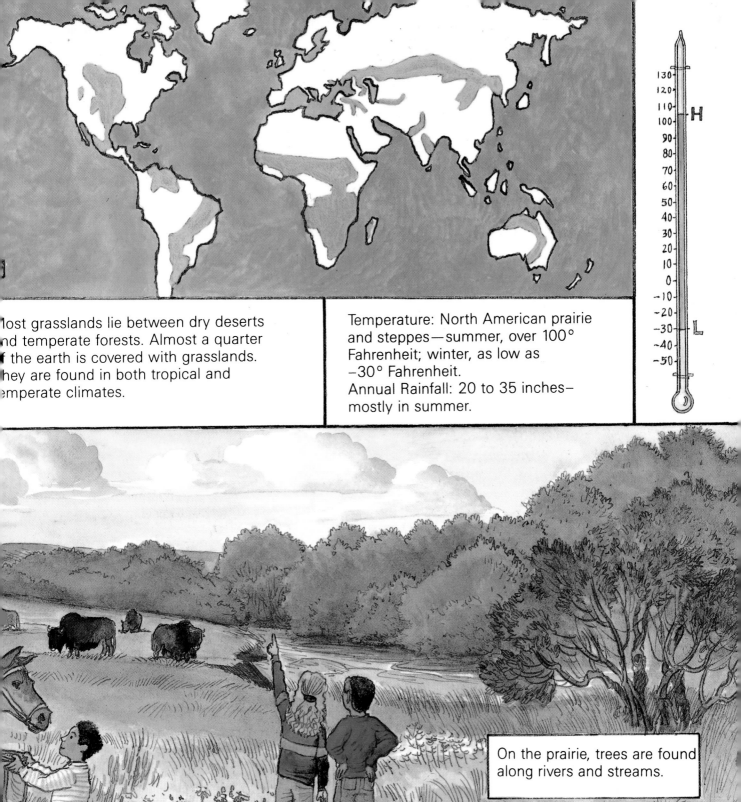

Most grasslands lie between dry deserts and temperate forests. Almost a quarter of the earth is covered with grasslands. They are found in both tropical and temperate climates.

Temperature: North American prairie and steppes—summer, over 100° Fahrenheit; winter, as low as −30° Fahrenheit.
Annual Rainfall: 20 to 35 inches—mostly in summer.

On the prairie, trees are found along rivers and streams.

27

Steppes of Eurasia

The world's largest grasslands, called the steppes, stretch from Siberia to eastern Europe. Winters are cold and long. Summers are dry and hot. The grasses here are shorter than those of the North American prairie.

Pampas of South America

The South American grasslands are called the pampas, which means plains. They stretch from the Atlantic Ocean to the Andes. Winters are milder than on the prairies or steppes.

Savannas of Africa

Tropical grasslands, known as savannas, cover two-fifths of Africa and large areas of Australia, India, and South America. The dry winter season may last for 5 months.

There are 9,000 kinds of grasses in the world. They keep the soil from eroding and provide food for animals and people. Here are some important grasses.

Corn

Wheat

Rice

Sugarcane

Bamboo

Timothy

In wet areas, grass may grow 10 feet tall.

THIS WAY TO FRESHWATER PLANTS

HALL OF FRESHWATER PLANTS

Many kinds of plants grow in or near ponds, lakes, and other bodies of fresh water. Some plants are microscopically small and simple, such as the algae that form a green scum on the surface of ponds. Others are more complex flowering plants and grasses.

Some plants, such as the bladderwort and elodea, live totally underwater and have no true roots. Others, such as the water lily, live partially above and partially below the water. Many, such as cattails and giant bulrushes, live in thick clumps along the water's edge.

Giant Reeds belong to the true grass family and can be as tall as 15 feet. Its feathery flower cluster can be 6 to 12 inches wide. Giant Reeds grow along the shores of ponds and lakes in water several feet deep.

Giant Reed

Look at all those fish!

Yes! And the plants provide oxygen in the water that fish need to live.

Bulrush

Bulrush grows in marshes or shallow water. Its tough round or triangular stems can grow 12 feet tall. It is used for weaving mats and for thatching houses.

Elodea

Bladderwort

Bladderwort is a carnivorous, vinelike plant with hundreds of little bladders on its stems that keep the plant afloat.

Duckweed is one of the smallest flowering plants. It is a favorite food of ducks and fish and has no stems or roots but floats on surfaces of ponds and marshes.

Water Lilies grow in both temperate and tropical climates. Air spaces in their tough long stem help keep them upright and carry air down to their roots. Leaves of the tropical water lily can be larger than 6 feet across. Flowers of some species are a foot wide.

Water Hyacinth is a free-floating flowering plant that may have as many as thirty-eight flowers on top of a stem. It multiplies rapidly, and huge mats of it can blot out sunlight and therefore the life of other plants and creatures below.

Mares' Tails look just like horses' tails. Their stems stand tall but their feathery leaves droop below water.

Elodea grows underwater and releases oxygen into the water.

Azolla is one of the small water ferns that float or root at the water's edge. The oxygen it gives out helps other plants to grow.

Mare's Tail

Water Hyacinth

Water Lily

Duckweeds

THIS WAY TO SALTWATER PLANTS

Azolla

31

HALL OF SALTWATER PLANTS

Many kinds of grasses and flowering plants grow along the shallow edges of the world's oceans. But the most numerous plants in the deeper ocean belong to the algae family. In fact, the first plants in the world were nonflowering algae that grew in the ocean. Today, algae continues to grow in both fresh and saltwater as well as on land.

Seaside Goldenrod

Sea Lavender

Salt-meadow Cordgrass

Sargassum Weed

Diatom is the one-celled alga that drifts in the plankton that feeds the creatures of the sea.

Irish Moss is an edible red alga that is also used for shoe polish and in shampoos.

Nullipore are strange-looking algae made up of little green plates. When they die, they crust over the coral reef and help build it. They were once thought to be animals rather than plants.

Mallows

THIS WAY TO
ANCIENT PLANTS

Giant Kelp

Salt-meadow Cordgrass grows
in shallow salt marshes and has long
flower clusters. Black ducks eat its
stems, and muskrats and geese eat
its roots. There are two kinds: one
grows to 2 feet, the other grows as
tall as 9 feet.

Sea Lavender is a flowering plant
that grows among sea grasses in
salt marshes.

Seaside Goldenrod has large yellow
flowers and grows as tall as 3 feet
along beaches and salt marshes.

Mallows grow 5 to 7 feet high in
salt marshes. A shorter form grows
to 3 feet high on the seashore.

Giant Kelp is a brown alga which
may grow as much as 18 inches in
a single day. This is the longest
plant in the world. It is food for
many sea creatures, including
whales. Kelp is also used for
medicines, ice cream, paints, and
animal and human food products.

Sargassum Weed is a brown alga
with air bladders that keep it afloat
in the waters of the Sargasso Sea.
The little sargassum fish looks like
the plant. Columbus was the first to
report seeing this plant, which is
sometimes called gulfweed.

HALL OF ANCIENT PLANTS

The earliest plants were single-celled algae that lived in the ocean about 400 million years ago. Plants appeared on land about 435 million years ago. These simple early plants had horizontal stems and upright branches with no leaves.

The first tree ferns appeared 300 million years ago. Parts of North America were covered with swampy forests of giant horsetails, ferns, seed ferns, and club mosses. When fossilized, these plants created the coal that is mined in the eastern United States today.

400 Million Years Ago

300 Million Years Ago

The first seed-bearing plants appeared 225 million years ago, when giant dinosaurs roamed the earth. Ancient conifers, cycads, and ginkgoes became plentiful. Toward the

200 Million
Years Ago

100 Million
Years Ago

end of that period the first flowering plants, called angiosperms, appeared. Those that could adapt and change were the ones that survived.

THIS WAY TO
HALL OF REPRODUCTION

HALL OF REPRODUCTION

Seedless plants such as fungi and ferns reproduce by spores, which form only when water is present. Later, when the spore cases ripen, spores travel with the wind and produce new plants.

Spore cases form on the underside of fern fronds and explode when ripe. Mushrooms develop spores on the gills under their caps.

Hey, look at all these spore cases!

SPORES

The most highly evolved plants reproduce by means of seeds. They develop from the sexual union of male and female cells. Like you, each plant is unique but has characteristics of its parents.

Botanists divide seed-bearing plants into two groups: gymnosperms (naked seeds) and angiosperms (covered seeds).

SEEDS

GYMNOSPERMS
(NAKED SEEDS)

Pine trees, spruces, and ginkgoes are examples of gymnosperms. Unlike ferns, gymnosperms do not need water to reproduce. For example, the pollen from the male pine cone is carried by the wind and lands on the female pine cone. When the female pine cone matures, it opens and drops seeds on the ground. A new plant begins.

Immature female pine cone

Mature female pine cone with seeds

37

Over time angiosperms came to dominate the plant world. Like gymnosperms, angiosperms are pollinated by the wind, but they also can be pollinated by insects and animals. In a typical flowering plant, new seeds form when the pollen from the male stamen is fertilized in the female pistil.

Once a flower is fertilized, many parts of it drop off as the ovary swells to protect the seeds within. The mature ovary is called a fruit and protects the seeds until conditions are right for them to grow.

ANGIOSPERMS
(COVERED SEEDS)

Parts of a Flower

Stigma (female)

Ovary
(female)

Pistil (female)

Stamen (male)

Pollination

Moving pollen from the stamen of one flower to the stigma of a similar flower is called *pollination*. Insects are the most common pollen carriers of angiosperms. Some flowers can be pollinated only by specific insects.

Plants pollinated by butterflies and moths.

Morning Glory

Phlox

Plants pollinated by bees.

Verbena

Larkspur

Plants pollinated by flies and beetles.

Sunflower

Poppy

39

VEGETATIVE REPRODUCTION

lthough most plants reproduce by seeds, ny plants can be multiplied by vegetative roduction. New plants can grow from ns, leaves, or roots. These plants are ntical to the parent plant.

Try this: Place a raw and unwaxed sweet potato in a glass of water. Use toothpicks to keep the top part of the potato above water. It should grow a green vine in a few weeks.

You can multiply plants with leaf cuttings.

You can multiply plants by dividing their stems or the entire plant.

African Violet

Daffodil

Begonia

Snake Plant

Hey, look! Roots are growing right out of these leaves.

New strawberry plants develop from runners called stolon.

New potato plants grow from underground stems.

THIS WAY TO THE MUSEUM SHOP

MUSEUM SHOP

All living things depend upon plants both directly and indirectly. Plants supply us with...

Oxygen

Sun provides energy for plants.

People and animals breathe out carbon dioxide.

Plants use carbon dioxide and energy from the sun to make food.

Plants give off oxygen. People and animals breathe in oxygen.

They also provide us and other living things with...

Food

We eat the roots, leaves, seeds, stems, fruits, and flowers of plants.

Leaves

Roots

Flower

Fruit

Stems

Seeds

Fruit and Nut Trees

We use the grain of grasses for bread, cereal, and pasta.

Sugarcane

Wheat

Rice

43

Fuel

Wood

Petroleum Oil

Gases

Coal

from fossil plants that lived millions of years ago

Clothing and Other Materials

Cotton Plant

Shirt

Thread

Rubber Plant

Tires

Sneakers

Hemp Plant— for rope

HALL OF FAME

John Bartram
1699–1777
A botanist who planted the first arboretum in the United States, near Philadelphia, in 1728. One of the earliest plant collectors in the United States.

Carl von Linné
1707–1778
A Swedish naturalist who created a system of classifying plants and animals and gave them all unique names in Latin.

Charles Darwin
1809–1882
An English naturalist who studied how plants evolve and survive by adapting to hazards of the environment.

Asa Gray
1810–1888
A botanist who specialized in classifying plant life in the United States.

Gregor Mendel
1822–1884
An Austrian monk who did experiments with garden peas to understand how organisms inherit certain characteristics from their parents. He is called the father of genetics.

Luther Burbank
1849–1926
A plant breeder who developed many new trees, fruits, flowers, and vegetables, including the Shasta daisy, white blackberry, and spineless cactus.

Margaret Ferguson
1863–1951
A botanist who studied petunias and challenged Mendel's experiments on genetics. Her findings were confirmed. First woman president of the Botanical Society of America, 1929.

George Washington Carver
1859–1943
An agricultural chemist who developed products from crops in the southern United States such as peanuts, sweet potatoes, and pecans.

Liberty H. Bailey
1858–1954
A botanist who developed agricultural education in the United States at Cornell University. He dealt with practical problems for farmers and gardeners.

Mary Agnes Chase
1869–1963
A botanist who continued the study of the grasses of the western hemisphere, and helped provide information to scientists working to develop nutritionally better and more disease-resistant crops.

Sir Alexander Fleming
1881–1955
A Scottish bacteriologist who discovered penicillin by accident while growing bacteria and fungi in his laboratory.

EXIT

THANK YOU FOR
VISITING THE
FLORATORIUM

Index

About the Contributors

Joanne Oppenheim, the author, has written more than thirty books for and about children. She is a senior editor in the Publications Division of the Bank Street College of Education in New York. A former elementary school teacher, she is the author of the Mrs. Peloki series, which was listed several times among the IRA Children's Choices. She also wrote *Have You Seen Birds?* which was selected as an outstanding Science Book by the National Science Teachers Association and the Children's Book Council and which also won the Canadian Children's Council Literature Prize.

S. D. Schindler, the illustrator, graduated from the University of Pennsylvania with a degree in biology. Since then, he has successfully combined his interest in wildlife and botany with his artistic ability. He has illustrated many children's books and has also contributed features for gardening magazines and journals. When he is not working on his art, he enjoys playing the piano, recorder, and harpsichord, having a game of tennis or squash, and gardening.

Catherine Eberbach, the science consultant, has a background in ornamental horticulture, horticultural therapy, and children's environmental studies. She is responsible for Children's and Family Programs at The New York Botanical Garden in the Bronx. She is also a Research Associate with the Children's Environments Research Group of the City University of New York. Her professional work includes designing children's gardens for discovery and play and speaking about children's perceptions of gardens and plants. Ms. Eberbach holds a B.S. in horticultural therapy from Kansas State University and an M.S. in public horticulture administration from the University of Delaware.